The Unseen Realm

Phil Campbell
The Unseen Realm

—

Published by - Spines
ISBN: 979-8-89569-631-6

This book is a work of fiction. All characters, places, and events portrayed within are products of the author's imagination. Any resemblance to real persons, living or dead, or actual events is purely coincidental. The views and opinions expressed in this work are those of the fictional characters and do not necessarily reflect those of the author or any real individuals.

The Unseen Realm

A Chronicle of Dreams, Warriors and Destines

P. E. Campbell

Contents

Introduction

Revelation 18:1-2

And after these things I saw another angel come down from heaven, having great power; an and the earth was lightened with his glory.

And he cried mightily with a strong voice, saying, Babylon the great is fallen, is fallen, and is become the habitation of devils, and the hold of every foul spirit, and a cage of every unclean and hateful bird.

Just The Way It Was

[Sam Narrates]

Sitting in his office at the end of his day Sam Hobbes contemplates the last 20 years and the recent events of his life and sipping his hot chocolate made with a mother's love with extra marshmallows, he thinks of the time that has passed since the last time he's seen his Uncle and his Dad his thoughts begin to flow into his mind as he tries to find the perfect time to take the next step.

Has it really been ... It's been 20 years since my Dad and my Uncle died.

Many people know the story but most don't;

For those that don't know ... some of the things that are about to be brought to light in this story might be shocking for most of you.

For some it might not be so shocking, for some it might sound like I'm losing my mind but I assure you that this is not the case.

My Mother (Gretta Milano) hasn't spoken much of it but I know there's more to what

happened, the gaps just don't add up.

My Dad was mentally challenged, he showed his love for me in many different ways (Art Hobbes) I miss him dearly and especially his PB&J's.

Also, My Uncle was framed for a murder that made him kill an innocent man.

I vaguely remember details from that night, I didn't know it at the time but it was the last night I'd spend with my Dad.

He would do anything to keep me safe, I've had dreams and visions since I was young and now that I'm an adult there are things that I understand now that I couldn't before ... and the one thing is certain, there is a spiritual world that overlaps our physical world.

Another thing that you should be aware of in this life, is that there is a physical world and that there is a spiritual realm and often time what happens in the physical realm manifests itself in the spiritual realm.

In the Bible when the disciples failed to cast out a demon, Jesus told them "this kind can only be cast out by praying and fasting."

In other words, you need to win the battle in the spiritual realm first before you can win it in the physical world.

Praying and Fasting are spiritual matters than can bring tangible results in the physical world.

And so with this understanding I want you to know when we're facing unexplainable difficulties, or what appears to be an abnormal trial we are in fact being attacked in the spiritual realm.

People can be possessed by demons.

People can be oppressed by demons.

Demons are cunning

They can have complete control over a one aspect of a persons life.

I believe more is hidden than is seen.

I'm not sure Uncle John understood that when he died.

My mom used to talk about these strange calls Uncle John used to get in the middle of the night and also about this sadistic killer named Edger Reese.

At the time Uncle John detained him he wasn't Reese he was possessed with a demon.

She also told me how my Uncle was responsible for his capture.

Before he was executed there was an exchange between Reese and Uncle John

but... she never gave me details about what that exchange was.

I never told my Mom about the visions and dreams that I have but I suspect she knows..

I see her praying daily, it's as if she's talking directly to someone who is close and not some entity far away.

I'm telling my part in this tale as a dedication to my Uncle to further his legacy.

My Uncle Detective John Hobbes was a very skilled and decorated lawman, who caught at least 8 top class criminals in his career.

He was also highly intelligent and cunning, able to fool Azazel, a demon much older than himself, into a trap.

there have been a lot of untrue things written and said about him, satire and misinformation and blatant lies have been fabricated by the media and I want to make sure that his death was not in vain.

This is the second night I've had a "visitor" shrouded in mystery come to me in a dream although I'm not sure I was actually sleeping.

This mysterious visitor would appear to me several times through the years with signs and visions.

I've often wondered why my Mom surrounded herself with Angels in our home sometimes staring at them while her thoughts drifted from her mind and she would often tell me about a war between Angels and Demons that plays out in our world.

She also told me that there were chosen people who live among us that have the capability to fight these demonic entities.

These entities...They are everywhere and nowhere, and they act always with vengeance.

If you can, do not let them notice you, or your life will be filled with regret.

They stalk those who prey upon them, therefore hide your good works.

Only those who are quiet and modest will avoid their attention altogether.

She also told me about how Azazel had the power to enter other people through touch and told me about a time she had to flee to a church because he tried to possess her.

My Mom used to tell me stories about her Dad who was also a Decorated Lawman Robert Milano and my Uncle and how Azazel did the same thing to both of them.

Robert and Uncle John's ending shared a lot of similarities

Once a demon joins with a human being, he acts along with

him using the logic of a man. Once inside they know you and remember.

Therefore they speak all the tongues of Babel.

The demon posses a form which allows him to be with humans.

In other words our country politically is in the hold of the top 5 demons in Hell.

She always use to say that my time would come and that when it did I'd have to make a choice.

To join the War or spend the rest of my life hiding from it.

I've always had concerns in the past about what I believe but lately there's been an uptick in demonic activity, and well... some things can't be explained.

Some reports have suggested that the new copy cat murders that have sprung up all over the city have more questions than answers.

The lines have been completely blurred between light and darkness, this is the beginning of a revelation that started 2 months ago.

The dreams I've been having lately seem very ominous last week I woke up sweating heavily clinching my fist. All I can remember is voices coming from the darkness and hands coming out of the darkness reaching for me.

I am Detective Sam Hobbes this is my story.

[Sam narrates]

This morning the "visitor" came to me in a vision.

Initially I thought it was just an angel all I remember was the light was very bright I could barely make out who or what it was.

This time... something was much different than the other times.

The voice sounded so familiar, it sounded like my Uncle John.

"There's a kid that needs your help Sam, when the time comes you're going to have to be there for him."

My phone immediately starts ringing ..it's Mom.

"Sam" she says. "Yes Mom" I reply.

"Are we meeting for dinner later ?"

(Sam Narrates)

Our weekly routine for so many years now.

"Yes mom I reply sort of swiftly as I'm running late to work."

"Detective Sam Hobbs" as I enter the precinct.

The voice again rings loudly in my head

This is the same riddle that drove my Uncle insane, the answer seemed to be connected

To my Mom and Robert Milano.

TIME ON MY SIDE?

The sun was setting gorgeously as I was taking the express way to meet with Mom.

My mind was racing as all of the thoughts from the previous visions were circulating while smooth jazz played in the background.

Diana's Restaurant was my mom's favorite (she loves the blueberry cobbler) we meet there at least twice a week to talk and catch up on current events.

Me and Mom used to have these conversations about Uncle John when I was young and she would tell me about how Uncle John didn't accept that this was spiritual war that we were in... which made him vulnerable to the attacks of Azazel she would also tell me that he was too proud of his accomplishments which drew the attention of the darkness.

She used to tell me on regular basis "Keep your good deed's hidden" I never understood why.

I can remember helping this girl after she had fallen off her bike and was trying to get back on it she was having trouble with her confidence and she couldn't even get back on the bike so I told her she could "do it" sort of like her personal cheerleader and she eventually got back on it and conquered her inner doubts.

This time however felt like there was more we had to discuss.

"Mom", I start ... this morning I had a "visitor" I start.

Mom says, well... and ? She says.

There was something different, it sounded like Uncle John.

Her face went blank as if she was staring into a memory from some time ago.

My cellphone vibrates ... "well aren't you going to answer that?" Mom said.

"It was my partner Det. Legacy Majors"

if the phone keeps ringing past 3 rings that means

it's important.

"Mom, excuse me" I said "I have to get this."

"Hey what's up?"

(Sam narrative)

My partner and friend Legacy was very near and dear to my heart.

She was adopted when she was very young; was an honor roll student by the time she got to Middle school and excelled all the way through school and straight to the Police Academy.

She was about 5'7 and Uber athletic.

Her sense of humor was very quick witted, shoulder length hair with a nose piercing.

When she dressed up she looked like she could win any beauty contest and when she dressed down she looked like the girl next door.

Her adopted parents would take her to church but she stopped going after one of the church's deacons was having an extra marital affair with one of the members.

She has never returned; she doesn't believe that the God of the Bible exist.

As she and her adopted parents went from church to church they would never truly settle on a church home, they eventually stopped going altogether.

When her adopted mother was tragically killed in a car crash, her adopted father never recovered and gave Legs back to the agency and checked himself into a psychiatric facility.

Legs used to tell me about these nightmares that she would have and how she sometimes felt afraid to go to sleep.

Growing up for her was rough in and out of foster homes never feeling a sense of belonging took its toll on her mentally.

Those struggles still linger even now..

"We got a call to check out a murder on the South side."

"Chief wants us to haul ass" she says. "Thanks Legs"

Majors was not only a very intense skeptic of spiritual matters; And also was one of my closest friends.

She thinks the "super natural" is a made up fantasy world in the same mold as Lord of the Rings.

She's often stated that "the Bible was written by men who made up stories to brainwash and control people."

(Sam narrative)

I hate that I had to cut me and Mom's dinner short but duty calls.

Mom I have to go I'll make this up to you I promise.

"Ok Sam" she said "make sure you stop by tomorrow please it's urgent."

"Yes Mom of course" I love you.

While I was driving down the interstate thinkin about this killer I'd caught last year and the string of copy cat murders that began. couldn't shake this feeling I was having, all the thoughts from the previous day were just so much more intense than what im comfortable with. What was so urgent that my mom wanted to share with me ?

I thought.

I think about my Dad and Uncle everyday.

The lessons that they've taught me still remain, and sometimes every now and then I can hear them speak. Voices of the past still echoing in my mind.

I think about what my Uncle used to say to me sometimes

"Something is always happening even if nobody sees it or understand it ....or accept it"

his voice echoing in my head as if he's sitting on my shoulder.

These voices are like pieces to a puzzle, I thought to myself.

If I could somehow manage to string them together maybe I could begin to make sense of them.

As I pull up to the station Lieutenant Hopson was already standing outside.

"Chief Hopson" I said. "We got a murder on 38th St. take your partner and go check it out". Lieutenant Hopson said.

He was being shorter than usual.

"Hey Chief you remember the copy cat killer from about 20 years ago Edger Reese"?

"Did he leave anything strange behind"?

I said. "Yea I remember" he said.

"Your Uncle John worked the Reese case my rookie year, even

though I was barely into my second year I didn't notice anything about him that stood out as concerning to me but I'd heard they used to say he was a narcissist and let some of the recognition he received and popularity go to his head and ended up dying in the woods on some psycho suicide mission".

"Reese left a documentary we did on him right before his execution."

(Sam narrates)

"Psycho suicide mission" ever since I was young everyone has always felt the need to share their opinions about my Uncle and what he did that fateful night.

When I was younger kids would tease me and tell me things that their parents would tell them about my uncle's death. "Hobbes was a murderer and karma got him in the end."

Kids can be cruel, so most of those years I spent alone until I met Legs.

I can still hear and remember my Uncle's voice from that morning, his voice ricocheted what he said before he left.

"No matter what people say about me, whatever I do... I'm doing because I love you".

Every time those kids would harass me with their words ..remembering what my Uncle's last words to me always got me through the day.

My Uncle Detective John Hobbes was a great man and I intend on continuing his legacy.

He believed cops were the chosen people, He believed he was saving the world from evil men like Edger Reese and others like him.

He was indeed just a man, and like every man he was flawed...

flawed in his thinking and his inability to understand what he was facing.

However, there has been a huge uptick in evil activity and demonic possessions.

Just the other day a woman reported a demonic attack at a church revival she was attending panic and terror was in her voice as I listened to the message from my radio.

She placed that call and it sent shockwaves through my unit but by the time some of us got there the lady claimed that the possessed woman had already left and that her body was found on the ground outside of her home, I guess time had run out for that poor woman.

Rumors of the same type of "copy cat" murders, more unexplained unsolved mysteries than I can count.

Riddles that connect to the same pattern to Edger Reese but he's been dead for 20 years, so how are these the exact same ? It's mind boggling to think how... the only thing that makes sense is...

My stomach suddenly gets an uneasy feeling as we approach the scene.

We turn down Michigan St. and head towards 83rd St. the familiar voice returned "whatever I do, I do because I love you"

(The car swerves)

Det. Majors says "another vision"? I reply "Yea... sorry"

"I tried to tell Mom today"... Legs interrupted "and we're here" Det Majors says.

Det Whitfield was standing next to the forensics expert looking extremely puzzled and confused. There were people standing off to the side with the obvious yellow tape that separated them from the detectives that were examining the scene.

As we approach Whitfield says “you guys ready to crap your pants?

What do we have ? “another copy cat” Stanton says.

“All left handed...like from before ...the Reese stuff” this just keeps getting more weird.

as he stood with a confused expression on his face.

The Fallen

A voice echoed in my head as if someone was intentionally trying to get my attention.

Then suddenly again "A Cop knows, a Cop sees... even the most casual thing.... it registers"

Det. Whitfield says aggressive (more aggressively)

HEYYY !! Hobbes !! "You with us??"

I answer "yea !! Yes !!" (Very hazily) "Sorry I drifted."

Whitfield shines his flash light next to the mirror behind the coffee table.

The hairs on the back of my neck stand at attention.

"Lyons (space)_____ Spakowsky" Whitfield says this is the 4th one this week.

"It's a riddle" I answer.

Suddenly my phone vibrated.

it's Mom. "I have to take this".

"Hey Mom" I answer.

"You know I normally don't bother you at work but I,"

"I'm already on my way Mom"

Sam was suddenly feeling very anxious about these developments and secretly looking for a way to escape, and Moms phone call provided him exactly that.

"ok see you soon i love you and be safe" "ok mom" the phone clicks.

I look at Det. Legacy and Whitfield.

"I have to go"

They both nod as they were both were still hypnotized by the riddle on the wall.

Legacy said skeptically "some weirdo is running around tryna be funny, nothing more Sam."

When I arrive at Moms place, she's standing by the door like she always does when she knows I'm coming over.

It's always nice to be greeted by Mom it reminds me of the first time I came to live with her. "Coffee and Hot cocoa" I say.

She responds with a slight giggle. "You know me too well" as we sit down at the table,

I start by saying "Mom... I think Azazel is back."

(Sam Narrates)

Her eyes gaze into a window of time that only she could see.

As if an old memory had resurfaced.

My Mom Gretta Milano was a retired theology professor, she adopted me after Uncle John died.

She told me years ago that Azazel wrote on my chest putting my life in danger which meant that my Uncle's death wasn't as suicidal as some have come to believe, it was more like a rescue mission.

He sacrificed himself for me, saved me ... and the result?

Whatever curse Azazel tried to put on me by writing on my chest is gone.

No trace of the letters, which is why my Mom had to tell me about it.

“Sam” she says. “Yes Mom” “there’s something about your Uncle you didn’t know.”

“I never told you” she continued. “When Azazel tried to enter him by touch, he couldn’t.

“She continued.

“Sam, before your Uncle died We had a conversation about the War between God,

Satan and about the Fallen Angels”

“I couldn’t get him to understand the meaning behind everything I was trying to tell him, but he really wanted to understand.”

“He read some of my fathers books and discovered Azazel could be killed.”

The war between God and Satan is as old as time itself, most of these evil demons have yet to reveal themselves.

(Sam’s Voice narrates

My Uncle John was a great Detective but he didn’t believe in God nor was he religious.)

“In my line of work faith is a little hard to sustain” she added.

“What I didn’t realize and maybe what he didn’t realize at the time..”

she pauses.

“He was one of the special people put here by God to fight against the demon Azazel”

(Sam narrative)

the hair started to raise on the back of my neck, The way my Mom’s eyes looked at me next I’ll never forget.

"Sam I believe you've inherited that ability from your Uncle."

(Both stares Intensely)

"What about the voices Mom"

I reply. "Voices ?" She says.

"Occasionally I hear voices that sound like Uncle John talking to me."

"When John died apart of him went into you Sam".

She continued.

"We didn't know it at the time but his sacrifice was saving us temporarily from Azazel".

The gaps of the story that never made sense before suddenly started to make sense.

She continued, "Sam... it's time for you to discover what you believe in".

(Sam Narrates)

Discovering what I believe in was what this was all about.

The possible return of Azazel, the copycat murders, and the uptick in exorcisms.

It was all connected somehow, same as my Uncle and the visions.

Is this a test?

My Uncle once said, there are moments that mark your life... I knew moving forward that this was that moment.

What I choose to believe was no longer something I could put off for another day.

This war against Azazel is in its infancy and it's not just one fallen angel, but Legions.

With a demonic agenda to steal, kill and destroy.

I started to wonder about our police chief and the men who were even higher up than him. Were some of them connected to all of this somehow ? One thing is for sure, all of the answers to my questions we're still being confirmed and there's was no doubt that the rabbit hole was about to get much deeper.

The uptick in demonic activity throughout this city has forced many people to lose hope, I can't ever remember it being this bad I remember seeing this story about a Mother who murdered her own son, and stuffed him in a suitcase during her trial she didn't seem to be remorseful or sad about what she had done.

She simply kept repeating she heard voices telling her to do it and that she believed it was Satan.

Seeing news like that leads me closer to this one conclusion Evil is intensifying and I can't put my head in the sand and ignore it.

My Uncle ultimately died to protect me, I'm apart of him and he was fighting against pure evil.

Time was running out, I couldn't afford to keep standing in the gray area about what I believed, battle lines are being drawn and things are changing and the stakes are being raised higher and higher daily.

I became a Detective but I'm more than just a "Detective" my Uncle didn't get to that truth, he died understanding he was protecting me and my Mom.

So it's up to me to continue where he left off, I used to be embarrassed by the things people would say about my Uncle.

They'd look at me right in my face and say "you're Uncle was a fool" "a coward" some would say.

It doesn't matter what they've said now, cause what he did, he did because he loved me.

Hell On Earth

My mind was racing triple time.

I'd never ever explored these thoughts of what I actually believed in before.

By now most of my hot cocoa was just about gone with the exception of some foam and a few marshmallows, I couldn't help but notice my mom and the look she had on her face.

It's as if she was gazing into that window of time that only she could see.

Maybe it was a distant memory of Uncle John; I always felt she cared about my Uncle on a much deeper level than she was allowed to express.

As she stared into my eyes her cell phone starts ringing.

"it's Dr. Shottah" she says gleefully.

(Sam narrative)

She had mentioned this guy to me some weeks back and told me she wanted me to speak with him about something urgent.

I was curious.

“it has been a while” Mom replies “I’d love to” she holds her hand up as if she already knows what I was going to say.

“Yes Dr. Shottah we will be right over”

I saw the joy return to my mom’s face and she smiled and turned to look at an angel statue that was next to her front door.

She always seemed to get inspired by those beautiful marvel sculptures.

She turns and says to me with a smile “let’s go there’s someone I’d like you to meet

“Dr. MaShaka Shottah, one of the world’s best and brightest scholars.”

His book “Goliath and the Nephilim” has been number 7 on the best seller’s list for 7 years.

He took an interest in my Mom and her story about my Uncle and Robert.

(Sam Narrates)

He was mainly known for a legendary exorcism that he did back in the 80’s that was said to have lasted an entire week.

Whispers of the rumor still persist until this day.

... some believe it was a hoax.

I haven’t read his book but I’d like to.

Since that point he’s written over a thousand books on demons and my Mom has even stated that she thinks my Uncle read one of his books before he made his stand against Azazel.

I was looking forward to this meeting with Dr. Shottah, there are things that need to be discussed and questions that need answering before I eventually make my decision on this whole Angels vs Demons, God vs Satan thing, one thing I know for sure... there are times that mark your life, moments when you realize nothing will be the same, and time is divided into 2 parts... before this and after this.

I told myself that no matter what I found out I would continue to move forward.

My cell phone rings... it was Detective Legacy.

"Hey, everything alright"? "The way you rushed out, I figured I'd check on you"

"Hey, I'm glad you called" I said. "I'm on my way to meet someone with Mom"

"I'll give you a call after Im done here" "alright she said.

Lt. Hopson got a lead and asked me to meet with some "Preacher" on the North Side" Detective Legacy replies.

As we pulled up Dr. Shottah was already waiting outside as we arrived.

There was a calmness that came over me it felt good to be with him and my Mom seemed to feel it as well.

"Dr. Shottah" my Mom says as they embrace.

"Please call me MaShaka" as they shake hands.

"This must be Sam." He says.

"Sam your reputation proceeds you, I've heard great things about you

I'm glad to finally have the pleasure."

(Sam's reply)

Thanks Dr. Shottah I reply.

"I've heard a lot about you as well."

"Do you have somewhere?"

Yes he says. "Follow me."

As we enter Dr. MaShaka's office that seemed to be shrouded in mystery the first thing

I notice is this book sitting on this amazing marble table I caught a quick glimpse of what the book's title was "Book of Wisdom" in bold letters across the front, and also an amazing painting by Legendary artist Gustave Doré from 1855 of Jacob wrestling with the Angel.

It was breathtakingly beautiful.

Dr. Shottah began speaking.

"There are spiritual beings in the world we live in, hiding disguised in human form.

There are real unclean evil spirits out there, real people who are genuinely and truly demon-possessed there is a quote that says the greatest trick the devil ever pulled was convincing the world that he doesn't exist.

This one trick has allowed him to operate as the God of this world working behind the scenes with most people entirely unaware of his influence.

Can you not see it? Look at the state of the world, wars and rumors of war,

common sense seems to have disappeared and people now call good evil, and evil good. realities of right and wrong have become distorted, demons are real and their influence is more pervasive than ever, yet society tries to bury this truth.

Even today there are events that transpire which we cannot simply explain away.

By dismissing the existence of the devil and demons we leave ourselves vulnerable, to their influence unable to recognize or combat the spiritual battles being waged around us."

Sam your Mom has spoken to you before about a war between this world and the spiritual world... correct? He asks.

Yes I replied... she has spoken to you of this many times.

So why do you seem unsure of what to believe (rhetorically)?

He asks.

He continued... "it's rhetorical."

you haven't decided what you believe in yes?

"I can't believe it" Sam says.

I thought ... "it's like this guy is reading my thoughts".

"That's correct Dr."

I replied.

He continued.

You're unsure of what you believe in particular because of what happened with your Uncle... John? correct ?

He asks.

I replied "yes, well it's complicated but I have a better understanding of the sacrifice my Uncle made when I was younger".

"This denial only strengthens their hold on the world, He continues. "I'm aware of what happened to John at the cabin in the woods".

"It was indeed a heroic sacrifice" John was a great man and I'm sorry that you lost him and your Dad". Thank you I replied.

He was fighting an ancient demon named "Azazel"

Yes Dr. that's correct I replied.

We've recently discovered there are more copy cat murders turning up ... some at the precinct have started to suspect that copy cat murders are connected with the murders from Edger Reese. "Edger Reese was possessed with Azazel his war against this world is only intensifying ?"

"That's correct Dr" I reply.

Hmmm interesting Dr. Shottah says.

Well Sam ... your Mom is right.

He continues ...

"The Book of Enoch brings Azazel into connection with the

Biblical story of the fall of the angels, located on Mount Hermon, a gathering-place of demons of old."

"Here, Azazel is one of the leaders of the rebellious Watchers in the time preceding the Flood from the Noah's Ark days; he taught men the art of warfare, of making swords, knives, shields, and coats of mail, and taught women the art of deception by ornamenting the body, dyeing hair, and painting the face and the eyebrows, and also revealed to the people the secrets of witchcraft, it was said that in those days that GOD saw the wickedness of man was great in the earth, and that every imagination of the thoughts of his heart was only evil continually.

the LORD regretted that he had made man on the earth, and it grieved him at his heart."

"Azazel is a very powerful demon and he is thousands of years old."

"There is a certain prophecy in Revelation 9 where a fallen Angel opens a bottomless pit that unleashes legions of demonic creatures on Earth and I think Azazel is searching for the key."

"He and his legion have been tormenting humankind through their demonic agenda ...

the fall of Babylon and this war plays out everyday in our physical world."

He continued.

"we do not wrestle against flesh and blood, but against principalities, against powers, against the rulers of the darkness of this age, against spiritual hosts of wickedness in the heavenly places. Therefore take up the whole armor of God."

"Hell is about to be unleashed on this earth, you cannot fight the fpdark forces of this war without the proper preparation and armor, the weapons of this war are not visible always with your eyes."

Ephesians 6:10-13

"In this passage, Paul revealed to us as believers that all the evil, wickedness, immorality, perversion, murders, violence, and evil that is increasing across the Globe is the result of demonic spirits working behind the scenes or what I would like to say, principalities operating through personalities that are yielded vessels for them to operate through. These are disembodied spirits looking for bodies to carry out their assignments of Hell on Earth."

"We see here that Paul (writer of Ephesians) begins to reveal that these demonic spirits are ranked as in the military has rank. He lists this rank as principalities, Powers, Rulers of darkness, and Spiritual Hosts of Wickedness in Heavenly Places."

First, we have "Principalities."

These are strong spirits that are assigned over nations and cities. Examples of these would be such as the "Prince of Greece" and the "Prince of Persia". Both of these were mentioned in the Old Testament and were strong spirits that hindered prayers, caused disruptions, and even attacked the people of God.

The next rank is "Powers" which seem to be spirits that are under the rank of these "principalities" that actually help aid them in their assignments. Then we have "Rulers of darkness" that appear to be chief spirits that empower people to carry out sinister schemes and evil on the earth.

These could actually be the spirits that influence and even possess world leaders in high positions that carry out evil, demonic, and sinister plans in high places even governmental positions on the Earth.

Then lastly, we have these "Spiritual Hosts of Wickedness in Heavenly Places".

These also seem to help aid the agents of the rulers of darkness to carry out assignments of hell.

I believe one specific spirit is now being unleashed with the intent to bring America down at her weakest point as a huge majority of Americans have turned from God and many in the Church have even been seduced by this spirit and that is a "perverse spirit".

Within the ranks of these spirits that we just mentioned from Ephesians, the bible indicates that there are certain spirits that appear to carry out specific attacks. For example, there is an Unclean Spirit, an Evil Spirit, a Spirit of Infirmity, a Lying Spirit, Seducing Spirit, a Spirit of Fear, a Perverse spirit, and a familiar spirit.

"but on the day that Lot went out of Sodom it rained fire and brimstone from heaven and destroyed them all, Even so, will it be in the day when the Son of Man is revealed"

"Sam the place your feet are standing on is Holy Ground always remember, you are safe from the enemy as long as you're resting on it."

My eyes were glued to every word he was saying.

"Dr ... do you believe these murders are connected with Azazel ?"

Meaning Uncle John didn't kill Azazel ?

Dr. Shottah begins. "Yes they're connected, And No.... somehow... Sam I believe John made an attempt to take Azazel on in a showdown and somewhat failed he only succeeded in protecting you and your Mom temporarily.

"All these years of the gaps not adding up has come to a crescendo".

The answer to the riddle I've wondered for years had finally come.

Sam narrative

My Uncle Detective John Hobbes died sacrificing himself for me, and somehow Azazel didn't die.

I looked at my Mom and I saw a single tear rolled down her cheek.

Her eyes glazed over as if she could see into some window of time that know one else could. Well one thing was clear from this meeting as suddenly all the doubts I had before I talked to Dr. Shottah melted away.

My Dad and Uncle were major reasons why I wanted to make a difference in this world and when they died they both left huge voids in my life. I never believed that I could make the Impact that I thought I was chasing it always seemed like an unrealistic expectation.

At one point, I didn't believe in a supernatural war between demons and humans that played out in our world.

We sat in Dr. Shottah's office in complete silence thinking on the things we shared with each other and staring at that picture of Jacob wrestling with the Angel and one thing became stunningly clear... most of the questions I've had about my Uncle were now being answered, there was no more room for excuses the time had come.

Now I believed.

Angels vs Demons

"Sam" Dr. Shottah turned and looked at me after calling my name

"Yes Dr"

I replied.

There is more we still need to discuss.

One of the main things I want to know about is the voices... your Mom told me about the voices you hear from time to time.

"Yes" I reply sometimes the voice sound like my Uncle."

I get so emotional sometimes that I lose my focus and sometimes doubt my purpose.

"This is it... this is your moment of truth" Dr. Shottah continued.

"It is foolishness to try to fight demons by your strength."

"Some of the weapons of this war can be fought with physical weapons but some cannot, Sam the most powerful weapon one can have is prayer but we will speak more about that later.

"This is about spiritual warfare Detective Hobbes.

Your Uncle didn't realize that, he didn't believe.

Even Satan sometimes can appear as an agent of Light.

He tempted Jesus with the all the glory and splendor and kingdoms of the world, all of the governments of this world are directly tied to Satan and his demonic agenda."

Dr. Mashaka Shottah was a student of the Bible he also had otherworldly faith and confidence in the scriptures.

"Your spiritual eyes haven't been opened, so there are things you can't see right now."

"Ultimately all I'm asking is for you to trust me."

He said to Sam.

"As you know, there has been an uptick in demonic activity and also copy cat murders similar from the ones of Edger Reese.

I think the demon Azazel has indeed re surfaced.

"what do you think is the endgame ?

Dr. Shottah asks. "Perhaps he is looking for someone" I reply.

"or for some thing, I think he wants to torment humans and cause as much chaos as he can."

that's mostly correct Dr. Shottah replies. "the great dragon was thrown down, that ancient serpent who is called the Devil and Satan, the deceiver of the whole world—he was thrown down to the earth and his angels were thrown down with him"

"The downfall of Babylon or in other words the destruction of our civilization every demon has a job Detective Hobbes."

"I think Azazel is causing as much chaos as possible but that's only a diversion".

"He is looking for something."

"Those jobs are the chaos that we see around us everyday.

"divorce, murder, theft, lies, confusion."

There is a demon behind every temptation and sin that has ever been committed."

Sam asks "So how am I supposed to fight them ?"

"You can't" he replied.

"If you only see the world through your physical eyes, you will be deceived."

He continued... "there is more than meets the eye Sam, things are not always as they appear" "this war that you are apart of is only partially played out in your world."

This war that Dr. Shottah speaks of has been fought for thousands of years before in eternity past.

Satan convinced a third of the Angels to rebel against God and Micheal the Archangel and the other Angels fought and defeated the rebellious legion out of Heaven banishing some to fall to earth and part of the punishment was most of them have no bodies just spirit form.

So it is here on earth that they're vengeance is played out against unassuming humans, blinded be social media and tv and other distractions that they have, This war was about a rebellion and one rouge Angel... Satan or Lucifer who wanted to be or thought he was like God.

So they began to corrupt the bloodline because of the prophecy of the Carpenter.

They vowed to destroy the blood so that his birth could be prevented

Meanwhile (Across Town)

Sam narrates

Detective Majors is answering a call from a Pastor at this new church with a very charismatic, young preacher named Shawn Stone.

Apparently, there is heavy demonic activity with reports of some needing to be exorcised. Pastor Stone graduated from H.S.

When he was about 14 years old and from there went to Dallas Theological Seminary.

He is widely popular with some even calling him the "Statesman of God" such gaudy titles raise huge red flags in my opinion. Det. Legacy isn't convinced he is sent from God or any other supernatural phenomena.

She is convinced that he is a conman.

The meeting between these 2 should be interesting.

"Pastor Shawn Stone" she Says as they approach each other for the first time.

"Det. Legacy" Shawn Stone replies as they shake hands respectfully.

I'm here in response to your call she says. "Ahhh yes Det. Right this way" fallen angels are angels who were expelled from heaven.

"Is that what you think this is all about ? Angels vs Demons?"

"Well yes Detective what else would this be about?"

During the late Second Temple period the biblical giants were sometimes considered the monstrous offspring of fallen angels and human women.

Yea so what does that have to do with the exorcisms coming from this area ? 'Open your eyes' he replies. '"look around sometime'

Legacy phone vibrates.

"Hey Sam, what's up."

"We got major things developing with Dr. Shottah", can we meet up ? "Yea she replies.

Im just finishing up with Pastor Stone."

I have to cut this shorter than I expected Preacher.

"What's the rush Detective ?" Stone says.

I'll be in touch Pastor Stone.

"I look forward to our next meeting Detective, we really could use your help i feel so overwhelmed."

Pastor Stone was a classic example of things not always appearing as they seem

He was surrounded by dark energy

She leaves hastily as Pastor Stone looks on sinisterly.

(Sam narrates)

Prepare for Glory

And the fifth angel sounded, and I saw a star fall from heaven unto the earth: and to him was given the key of the bottomless pit.

And he opened the bottomless pit; and there arose a smoke out of the pit, as the smoke of a great furnace; and the sun and the air were darkened by reason of the smoke of the pit.

Sam being bombarded with images and voices had yet to put the pieces to the puzzle together the only thing he could think of was Dr. Shottah, full of knowledge and wisdom certain MaShaka could help him put together the pieces that would make it easier to decode.

He thought about his Uncle and the books that he read the night before his meeting with Azazel, he thought his mother and the brief encounter that ended with her fleeing into a church. Sam's thoughts were circulating around him vigorously.

Stories he would hear as a youth briefly emerged and replayed like the story of the man who was possessed that lived in the tombs that Jesus confronted and was healed and freed from those demons. There was this story I read a few months ago about a kid named Shad and how he was getting beaten and bullied at school cause he would talk to other kids about Jesus and the Bible.

(Sam Narrates)

I arose with sense of urgency because of those words that echoed in my head ... had I dreamed them ? Who were they coming from ? Once again more questions than answers. There was only 2 people I felt comfortable enough talking about this to, and one of them is probably sleeping.

"Hello Sam, what do I owe the pleasure of this phone call ?".

Dr. I just had the craziest vision and I was hoping you could tell me what it means... is there somewhere we can meet ? Yes Sam I'll text you my exact location said Dr. Shottah.

On the way to Dr. Shottah's mysterious man cave.

I started thinkin about the vision, I saw a shadowy figure standing next to some sort of black hole or pit with a key

the vision seems to get blurry after that.

Also kept having the overwhelming feeling that my mom was keeping something from me.

As I approached, the detailed security that Dr. Shottah had was incredible and there was always a white and greenish light vibrating through these security beams.

The positivity that was radiating from this place was incredible.

There wasn't anyone that was ever gonna sneak up on this guy.

I had to keep reminding myself that this guy was a Theologian and not a Gazillionaire.

As I enter into the main hall Dr. Shottah meets me as i

approach the smell was the sweetest fragrance that put my whole body at ease.

We enter this room full of all these awesome paintings.

There was a huge mosaic rug that had a few different shades and a couple different colors of paint that were different from each other.

"So Sam" "I hope you're enjoying this exclusive tour of my personal chambers."

he says... "why have you summoned me to this meeting." he says.

Well Dr. as I stated before I need help interpreting these visions and it seems like you're the only one that can help me with that.

Ok Sam... I'll do the best I can please, have a seat get comfortable you're quite safe here.

The vision has been the same, it's a shadowy figure standing next to a black hole pit type of darkness.

Is he holding a key ?" Yes!! I reply. "Sam, God has given you a vision of Revelation 9.

"You have the gift of foresight"

"What am I supposed to do with this gift Dr. ? "Join the fight Sam" Dr. Shottah replies.

How ? These are forces I don't yet understand?. "You are not alone Sam." I'm not ?

I thought. "Sam ... follow me" he walked over to this button near his desk and pressed it.

A door opened and he walked through "Sam ... are you coming ?

As I followed the Dr. down this long bright corridor he begins to speak to me again.

"Sam your Mom has been preparing you for this moment for a long time we have had conversations about the war and about her encounter with Azazel, she has a very special ability to help others the way she helped you Sam when you were a very small child was her displaying the love of God... that ability is rare in these days and times, our meeting isn't accidental. Not by chance or circumstance, this was destined to happen according to our Lord's timing. Shottah says.

"We've arrived." Dr. Shottah says

Another door opens it's beaming bright with a white and greenish tint... he hands me what looks like high tech safety goggles

Sam put these on please. Shottah says.

As we enter this room it was breathe taking.

There was what looked like scripture written all over the walls and a case was in the middle of the floor and it looked like it was housing something very Important.

This was no ordinary man cave.

Dr. Shottah continued "Sam, you are here for a very special reason, that reason brought you to me I suspect your mother knows this as well that's why she wanted us to meet.

You have a rare gift and in this battle that gift is very valuable to both sides;

The key is to discover what this gift is and harness your true purpose.

You have to forget what you think you know, this is a spiritual war between the forces of darkness and of light."

"As he finished his sentence he reached his hand into a case and pulled out what appeared to be the most glorious sword I'd ever seen."

The structure of this sword was legendary, it almost looked as if it was made with fluorescent glass. At the tip of the blade was crimson red like blood.

On the handle was transparent gold and transparent silver and glowing very bright.

There was writing around the base of the handle but it's inscription was too small from me to make out what it said.

"This is Shekhinah."

She has seen many battles, and is God's vengeance against the wicked ones." He said.

Im beginning to get the feeling there is more to who Dr. Shottah is than I initially thought.

His whole vibe is otherworldly.

I wondered how many times he had used it, or if he had ever used it, or was he some kind of guardian or protector ?

I was speechless. "Dr. Shottah ... are you able to wield that ?"

He held it in his hand and it came to life as if he'd become one with it and it one with him. "Sam, do not be afraid".

"Our enemies are gathering and searching for a key that will open up the bottomless pit prophesied in Revelation 9.

"There has been an uptick in demonic activity all over the world."

This battle is intensifying we have to be preparing for what's coming Sam."

They will come for you and everyone you love how long will you stand trapped in the middle ?

As I looked at Dr. Shottah ... light ... pure light was vibrating all around him.

"The spirit world governs the physical world" "The Lord has chosen you" he said.

then suddenly just as quickly as it was revealed it was gone.

His hand withdrew from the case and that same case that was glowing green and white light went dark. “Dr. Shottah will you help me ?

“I’m a Detective but I need you to be my eyes and ears to the street so to speak,

so what’s our next move ?”

“The first thing I need you to do” Dr. Shottah said.

You still need to consult with your Mom ... she has something important she still needs to tell you and you have something important you need to tell her... and then... we begin.”

(he looks at Sam confidently)

The Peacemakers

Dr. Shottah begins, "Gretta, it is important that you tell Sam how important he is."

"Yes I understand it's hard ya know… she replies.

I've shared so much with you after his Uncle died".

"I must go" we will continue another time Dr. Shottah hangs up.

[Sam Narrates]

She likes to keep her Angels spotless … so when the sun comes through her drapes they glow in the light of the day.

She is full of wisdom and strength, her confidence comes from the word of God.

praying daily, "Lord thank you I know that you always hear me."

"Lord please give me the strength to do your will, and help Sam find his way to the light of the truth.

"Her powerful prayers always seemed to shake the foundations of our house.

Weeks after my Uncle died, she held on to hope longer than I did ..that he was coming back.

I used to watch her sit by this window for hours when she wasn't aware that I was watching. Even though biologically she wasn't my mother I'll always love and take care of her as such.

She's taught me so much and there is no way I could repay her back for taking me in on such a short notice.

When I was growing up going to school sometimes was a nightmare.

The things people would say to me would sometimes hurt so bad id go home and cry silently for hours.

Silent tears hurt the worst, hurting inside while hiding it from my mother became a daily exercise, By the beginning of my Freshman year in High School I was a pro.

I saw my mother change from shy and timid to bold and fearless.

This transformation started about 10 years ago, she began to lock herself in her room and while she was in there she would pray.

I wasn't allowed to disturb her, I wasn't allowed in.

All I could do was wait for her to come out and when she did she was radiant.

It was almost frightening how she would look when

I would see her as I was hiding hoping she didn't notice, but I often wondered if she knew

I could see her.

Greta Milano was fighting a war in a unseen realm, and she was preparing me to stand alongside her.

I remember reading about this kid a few months ago

This kid would repeatedly get picked on and bullied at school but the reason wasn't a usual... he got bullied and beat up for sharing his love of the Bible.

I could definitely relate to that I took an immediate liking to that kid even though I'd never been introduced to him.

The voice in my head began "whatever I do, I do because I love you"

"Sam" Mom said. "Are you alright ?"

Sam replies.

"Yes Mom, remember the lil boy i was talking to you about a few weeks ago ?"

"The one that got beat on and bullied all the time ?"

"Yes Sam" she replies. "What about him?"

I hurried out of the door and into my car "Mom I'll call you later, I have some things to sort out." I reply.

As I rushed from her home to my car I began driving away in heavy thought, storm clouds had begun to form over my car which was very symbolic of the brainstorming that was taking place in my mind.

Blessed are the Peacemakers

(Sam narrates)

Sometimes I think the basic job of human beings is just to figure out what the hell is going on.

Sitting alone in my car it begin to rain.

The rhythm from the drops of rain put me into deep thought.

I needed help with my faith I need to learn about my salvation through Jesus.

Images of my Uncle begin to fill my head tears begin to fill my eyes.

Suddenly my phone vibrates... I answer. "Hello ?"

"Detective Hobbes" I wipe the tears and gain my composure.

"Jesus is the Son of God" "He died for the sins of the world" I reply who is this ?

"For God so loved the world that he gave is only begotten Son.

"That whosoever believes, shall not parrish but have everlasting life.

"I suddenly had a peace come over me, soothing and calming I asked "I want to believe in Jesus, I want to give myself over to his will" I replied.

The Angel continued... "It Is Written" "For whosoever shall call upon the name of the Lord shall be saved."

"Blessed are the peacemakers, for they will be called the children of God."

"It is only those who daily conquer sin in their own lives—who work to bring peace to the civil war in their own hearts—that are ready to help others fight this battle as well."

The voice went silent after these words. "Hello?" "Hello?"

There was silence.

On the way home I usually have some smooth jazz stuff playing in the background or some quiet storm playlist to soothe and calm me after a long tough day, but tonight was different.

Tonight there was no background instrumental, no playlist or noise and I was as calm as a newborn baby resting in its mothers arms.

I thought about my Mom and Dr. Shottah, also the choices that lie behind me as well as the ones that lay before me and everything that was going on it definitely felt like a crossroads moment.

As I pull up to my house.

grabbed my jacket from the back seat and notice a bible underneath my jacket.

I thought to myself "how did this get here ?"

I scooped it up along with the rest of my things and took it inside.

As I lay on the bed a bright beaming light began to shine, completely catching me off guard

it was so bright that I couldn't look upon it,

I shielded my eyes best I could.

The light was soooo bright but Honestly I was afraid to look at whoever or whatever was the reason for this.

This blinding light was similar to the light that Sam saw when he encountered Dr. Shottah's sword.

This light came directly from the Lord which was the source of this Angel's power.

"Don't be afraid" a voice said.

"Who are you ?" I replied.

"I am Michael one who intercedes between God and humanity."

"One who commands the army of angels loyal to God against the rebel forces of Satan."

"Go and speak to the Old man he has a special message designed for you."

(Sam Narrates)

I was frozen from what I was experiencing.

The Angel Michael was appearing to me and it wasn't a dream or a vision!

It was happening in real time.

I was afraid ....and certainly fearful of what was taking place.

This amazing light felt warm and comforting but also felt overwhelming and the Angel felt very set apart from anything in this world.

When Mom used to read to me from the Bible she would

sometimes read about how some of the people in the "stories" would encounter these heavenly beings. And the first thing they would say is "fear not" I used to always imagine what it would be like to have an encounter like that. Well wonder no more my body naturally was struck in a sort of awe and euphoric state.

Michael had one final message and then he vanished.

"Sam Hobbes, chosen of the Most High don't you be afraid."

The Old Man

(Sam Narrates)

There's an old man that everyone calls "Pop" i pass on my way to the office everyday.

I usually stop to check on him every morning.

Considering what happened last night I was looking forward to meeting with him and hearing his wisdom.

The mysterious thing about this old man is nobody knows his real name (I've heard many referring to him as "Pop") or why he was so wise, rumor has it he made a prophecy about a demonic invasion that led to him being ostracized from his church and his job. He was blackballed from his professional career nobody wanted to work with him.

All the years I've known him and I cannot get him to disclose his name.

There was this time he was telling me about this choir he was wanting to sing with but they kept telling him he was too old to sing with them and how it hurt his feelings and that an Angel told him that when he gets to Heaven he wouldn't have to worry about that happening he said the Angel told him that they would sing the most beautiful songs that human ears have never heard.

He didn't have any degrees as far as I knew the guy didn't graduate High School.

I've known him for at least 3 years and I don't know how old he is.

Maybe I really don't know him as well as I think I do.

(Jokingly)

As I pull into the alley where he usually is sitting by the dumpster I noticed he wasn't sitting there.

The rags and cart he uses was there "maybe he went to the restroom" I thought.

I waited there another 10 minutes when I noticed him walking down the alley.

"Hey Pop"

I greet him. "Well hello Mr Detective. "He responded."

As we shake hands I noticed there was a certain familiar feeling about him, Unlike any other time before.

"I've been walking with the Lord for over 40 years, but it seems as if I've seen more wicked happening in the last few weeks than I've ever seen."

"Many people today including young people, are drawn to occult practices like ouija boards and tarot cards and witch craft thinking it is just a game but these practices are not games they are real and dangerous pathways to the spiritual world and those that engage with them are opening themselves up to spiritual attack.

"There are countless stories of people who've experienced supernatural phenomena, after playing with ouija boards or engaging in occult activity. These are not isolated incidents or

Urban legends they are real accounts of people who have opened themselves up to the spirit world and had to deal with the consequences."

"These demonic entities do not fear us as individuals, they're not frightened by our worldly knowledge or our wealth, or physical strength."

What truly instills fear in these malevolent beings is the Lord, his power his majesty, and his authority over all creation both seen and unseen."

"While the Bible confirms the reality of sinister spiritual forces, it also promises us victory through faith in Jesus Christ."

"The Lord will always protects his children."

He also had a really nice singing voice and every now and then he would burst into song.

On a few occasions birds have been known to circulate whenever his sweet notes filled the atmosphere.

(He sings an impromptu song Just another day that the Lord has kept me)

"These last and evil days are getting darker, I never thought I'd live long enough to see it get this bad He said.

"By taking up His full armor, praying against strongholds, and interceding for people and places impacted by evil spirits, we can advance God's Kingdom into the strongholds where principalities operate."

Pop's face shines with wisdom and he always had a way of making me see things in a way that I never thought possible.

He always had this bottle of ointment that he kept close to him, he was short not even six foot, full beard and it was white. His hair was short and well groomed for a man who didn't have regular access to a barber. He always wore this shirt that said

"Messiah" and underneath in smaller letters it read "King of Kings."

His words seemed very ominous.

"What's on your mind young man, it must be something extraordinarily important for you to track me all the way down here" "well sir, I had quite an encounter last night."

I responded.

"You were visited by an Angel of the Lord."

"I knew it as soon as I saw you" the Old man replied.

I was shocked !! How did he know ??

I remained silent.

He continued.

"The Lord told me that you would be here today".

"He told me that you was ready to commit your life to him and be a instrument of peace for his glory." "Yes sir that's true." I replied.

"But I .... But I"

the Old man looked sternly at me and said.

(Sam narrates)

as he begin to speak a light came down from the sky and shinned on that Old man.

"Young man, God is not confined by the laws of physics like we are, you see he exist outside of space and time."

"In other words, his ways are not ours."

"You must learn to put on the full armor of God"

"when darkness and shadow is near you must not have doubts or fear or they will feed on it and use it against you."

"The spirit world is real, our actions in this reality impact what happens in the spiritual realm." He continued.

"Believers have the power to resist demonic principalities through faith in Christ's victory over them."

"These days are evil, and that very evil is growing stronger each day, but the Lord will always protect his children and that's why you and I are here." "Christ has disarmed these evil spiritual rulers and authorities through his death and resurrection (Colossians 2:15).

Sir what must I do to be saved ?" I replied.

"Believe that Jesus died for your sins young man, and you will be saved."

The Old man answered.

I got down on my knees right there in that alley and asked the Old Man if he would pray with me.

"I'd be honored son." He began.

"Lord you know Sam's heart, you said in your word that if you confess with your mouth that Jesus is Lord , and shall believe in heart your that God raised him from the dead thou shall be saved. "Sam do you believe ?" "Yes"

I replied. "Lord, I know you always hear the prayers of your children, bless the mission that you've set before my brother continue to shine your light of truth on him and guide his steps.

"Blessed are those who put their faith in you Amen."

When I opened my eyes, I felt a calmness that was peaceful and heavenly.

I'd surrendered myself to the Lord and had zero intention of turning back.

The Wise Old man appeared anticipating something, he was extremely silent.

"I feel different" I told him.

"No matter what happens, do no allow any doubts or negative feelings to enter your mind"

"Be strong in the Lord, Sam."

Suddenly there was a gust of strong wind swirling around where we were standing.

Looking at this Wise Old man stand fearless somehow gave me more encouragement to stand against whatever was approaching.

But what was is ? was it Azazel ? Or something else ?

The light that encompassed us appeared to be fading and the darkness surrounding us appeared to be growing more intense.

Then a voice pierced from the darkness

"You have no power here Old maaaaan", "stop talking nonsense"

"Your God has forsaken you"

"The darkness is coming, he is coming"

(Unknown Demon)

Looks at Sam "Ahhh well look who we have here ...Detective Hobbes, you have something we want."

Give it to us without hesitation and you may walk away with your life."

Sam narrates

What was it that I had that this ... thing wanted ?

Did it have something to do with what Dr. Shottah said about my Mom having something to tell me ?

Then suddenly the light that shone brightly was gone.

A shadowy darkness covered the alley where we were standing.

I'm not exactly sure how Pop knew what he knew about me.

It seemed like between him and Dr. Shottah they share the same wavelength.

I felt a negative presence fill the air.

Pop turned to me “We are told to pray against spiritual forces in the heavenly realms and make our requests known to God as evil is pushed back (Ephesians 6:12,18).

“Sam, stand your ground, a warrior of God is not a person who seeks out conflict, nor do they fight every battle they see.”

(Sam narrates)

He held a bottle of oil of some sort but I wasn’t sure about the substance inside.

“They listen to the Holy Spirit so that they know when they are to fight and when they are not.

Spiritual positioning is their center of operations.”

(Sam narrative)

As I he began to pray this Old man was incredibly impressive it was hard not to be in awe of him.

“Depart from us, you evil doers” he said sternly.

He didn’t seem worried that some type of evil presence was circulating around him.

As the darkness got heavier and the air became more foul.

Dominion and Power

He kills people who don't follow Antichrist (Revelation 13:15)

"He was permitted to give a spirit to the image of the beast, so that the image of the beast could both speak and cause whoever would not worship the image of the beast to be killed."

And the Lord said to me: "The prophets are prophesying lies in my name.

I did not send them, nor did I command them or speak to them.

They are prophesying to you a lying vision, worthless divination, and the deceit of their own minds."

Jeremiah 14:14

For such persons do not serve our Lord Christ, but their own appetites, and by smooth talk and flattery they deceive the hearts of the naive.

Romans 16:18

The Old man replied

"Greater is he that is within me, than he that is within this world."

"We stand on Holy ground"

"For we wrestle not against flesh and blood, but against principalities, against powers, against the rulers of the darkness of this world, against spiritual wickedness in high places."

"You have no dominion here demon."

The shadowy darkness replies.

"Shut up Old fool we've beaten you and others before, we are everywhere for we are Legion.

You're outnumbered.

These Dark entities didn't seem very intimidated by what the Old man was saying but neither was the Old man.

(Sam narrates)

I was absolutely shocked by what I was witnessing, the Old man was standing toe to toe with a demon, who appeared to be strong, and very powerful.

Then suddenly, a blinding light shines from the sky and a loud trumpet sounded from the sky above and by the time I could see who was standing next to me and the Old man the demon started shouting.

"Ahhhh the light is blinding us and BURNS !!! Take it off!!

Why are you here ?

Turn it off or you will kill us !!"

The Light Watcher spoke "Quiet ! demon of the fallen ! The rebels were defeated and cast down from Heaven; Satan is on borrowed time and it is short, we do not fear evil ..leave this place now."

"You can't harm Sam nor this Old man any time soon."

The darkness that had consumed the area we were standing in was suddenly gone.

The voice disappeared with the shadow.

What replaced that darkness was An amazing light show that I'm finding very difficult to put into words.

I could barely see what was going on so I depended on my ability to hear what was happening.

When I looked at the Old man, he seemed calm and confident as he looked back at me and said "Young Man, pray for my strength I don't know who that Agent of Light was but I'm sure glad you was here with me."

"The fellas down at the bingo hall aren't gonna believe this."

He said with a slight giggle as we both smiled at each other.

Then suddenly the Old man collapsed right there in the alleyway "it's alright Sam" he said with a gentle smile as his eyes were closed slightly "My time has come and gone like the sun, there's another who will join you on your quest I can't tell you when but from what I can see in my mind ... small child filled with the love of Christ." Then suddenly with a tear rolling down his cheek a light from heaven shines on him as if he is being welcomed by a heavenly force. "I have fought the good fight of faith and I've finished my course."

He closed his eyes and died right where Sam had been meeting with him for years. Sam was frozen as all the memories from they're time talking and knowing each other came rushing back to his mind, tears began to swell up from his eyes in a way this Old man took his Dad and Uncle John's place and was the closest thing to a family member.

As I made my way towards my car a zillion thoughts were going through my head.

What kinda Angel was that with me and the Old man in the alley ?

I'm certain it was and why did he seem so familiar ?

Just as I began wrestling with these thoughts my phone began to vibrate.

"Hey stranger" it was Det Legacy.

She has the uncanny ability of calling me when I'm in my deepest thoughts.

"Legs, you won't believe what just happened."

She quickly interrupted.

Which was oddly unusual for Legs.

"You won't believe that weirdo Pastor Stone I met with"

"Listen, this guy gave me the most seriously creepy vibes and I'm not going back there alone."

(Sam dialogue)

"You mean to tell me you guys had nothing in common ?" I reply sarcastically.

(Legs dialogue)

"Very funny Sam, seriously... this guy seemed off."

Legs says. "I'm pulling up to get you."

"Sam there's something about you... are you alright ?"

"I feel great Legs, honestly I've never felt better."

"Will you please stop looking at me like that."

She continues "Sam, Hopson has been smothering me ever since we left 38th.

"We need to go see Pastor Stone now and report back."

"Ok Legs, let's go."

We get in her car and as we begin to head down the road, she begins to fill me in about Pastor Stone and his "ministry"

"Sam, one of the possessed victims was a member of Pastor Stone's "Church".

This young woman had only been attending there a few weeks."

"Reports began to surface after a "revival" Pastor Stone had begun encouraging people to use Ouija boards and tarot cards, a new Age of Enlightenment he calls it.

Video of this event has gone viral."

With many claiming that Stone is some kind of "prophet."

"Legs, remember those conversations about God and Satan and the end of the world ?"

"Yes" she replied.

What does that have to do with Stone and this case ?"

(Sam narrates)

I pause and thought to myself "everything" but I remain silent.

"I think it's connected Legs.

"if we deny or doubt the evil that the Bible teaches ... it blinds us from seeing the truth about what we are facing."

"We don't only live in a world with just humans... but with spirits."

"Whatever" she replies "we're here".

(Sam narrates)

As we walk up to Stone's office I had a feeling that Legs really didn't want to be there. She seemed extremely nervous.

Pastor Stone opened the door before we even had a chance to knock.

"Ahh Detective Legacy you've brought company."

"This is Detective Sam Hobbes...Pastor Stone" She replies.

I reply "it's nice to meet you Pastor"

"Likewise Detective" Stone replies.

"Please, Please come in and have a seat make yourself comfortable." Stone says.

There was a certain uneasy feeling that surrounded this Pastor

He had dark energy that followed him.

"Let's cut right to it Preacher."

Legs wasted no time. "You preached a message a few days ago."

"Are you aware of the possessions people have reported to have had since your last sermon ?" "Aren't you supposed to be trying to free people from these negative things ? Instead it's as if you're helping to perpetuate them."

"Why no Detective" Preacher Stone says i am not aware of any such things, my members are living their ..best lives"

"Pastor Stone... do you take demonic possession lightly ?"

Legs asks.

"No Detective, I'm well aware of the seriousness of the matter, you seemed to be confused about what type of Church this is Detective are you a believer ?"

"We will be asking the questions Preacher !"

Legs responded obviously irritated.

"Legs ! I had to step in" "I'll take it from here"

"Was it something I said ?" Pastor Stone responded.

"It's been a long couple of days, why don't we start with something more simple."

Pastor Stone for some reason wanted to talk to Detective Legacy.

"It's ok Hobbes, I like Detective Legacy she has not offended me."

He continued. "Well Detective ? Are you a believer ?"

She replied sternly. “No” “I don’t believe in some dusty book that’s been more divisive than any other book in existence.” “Nothing in that book but myths and fairy tale stories”

“I don’t believe one man could be responsible for the whole world’s sins and die and be raised again.”

Stone slightly agrees.

“I think that dusty old book highlights the wrong good guy, I’ve always been intrigued by the serpent and how he was able to get Adam and Eve to eat from the tree of Knowledge.”

He continued.

“Det. Legacy you certainly can relate with this part of the story.”

(Sam narrates)

Me and Legs usually had these types of conversations privately all the time

I couldn’t help but notice the look on Pastor Stone’s face.

He seemed to be smirking at the fact that Legs wasn’t a believer almost as if he had been anticipating this.

I could see the wheels in his head turning but what could he be thinking ?

There’s no way I could let him know that I was noticing something so I kept my vibration low just like the Old man taught me.

(Uncle John's voice echoing..a cop sees, a cop knows ...even the smallest details it registers)

Things were escalating quickly the current events of the past few days were like a snowball going downhill.

Legs and Pastor Stone volleyed questions and answers back and forth for another 5 minutes the details of what was said was pretty obvious with Legs appearing more annoyed than anything.

Pastor Stone had a strange reaction when we shook hands

earlier how I felt in his presence reminded me of being back in that alley with that shadow.

That's when I noticed it, directly over the top of the doorway

"Revelation 13:15"

I'd heard of the book of Revelation before but I was a brand new believer

Who was basically a novice when it came to discerning what scriptures were supposed to mean.

In other words, I have no clue what that verse meant.

Bible verses always seemed so vague to me before.

But this... this was something different I knew if I could somehow connect this verse with the current events of what was happening it could be a game changer.

The hairs on the back of my neck begin to raise once again as I looked slowly, anxiously awestruck in the moment with more questions than answers.

"He was permitted to give a spirit to the image of the beast, so that the image of the beast could both speak and cause whoever would not worship the image of the beast to be killed."

The Boy | The Dreamer

And it shall come to pass in the last days, saith God, I will pour out of my Spirit upon all flesh: and your sons and your daughters shall prophesy, and your young men shall see visions, and your old men shall dream dreams:

(Sam narrates)

This morning there was a story I came across that had me feeling sick to my stomach.

A pizza delivery driver was robbed and murdered.

The arresting officers Nick Alvarez and Chris Occon seemed visibly upset about what happened.

One of them gave the following statement.

"Here you have a guy who was just trying to provide for his family and this happens, all you wanna know is Why ?"

"It's gruesome and demonic" the other one said.

"This person, you know, you always say the word 'evil,' but this is truly demonic."

The sheriff said the victim and suspect did not know each other, and there was no apparent beef before the encounter.

"There doesn't appear to be any relationship," the sheriff said.

"All it appears is that there was a gentleman who was working, was doing his last delivery of the night, and this person killed him for no reason.

And it took him away from his family."

Deputies have arrested notorious criminal Adrian Oscar Silas Jr. (who was just released on parole)

Authorities said they found human remains in trash bags behind the house where the suspect was staying.

Deputies believe Silas, 30, robbed and murdered Baker at the home.

Adam Baker is survived by his wife and 3 girls

(Sam narrates)

A few months ago I came across a story about a boy who claim to have dreams from God but he didn't know what they meant.

The reporter who was interviewing the Boy seemed to be unfairly portraying the boy as liar and made him seem like he was exaggerating the whole thing.

I can only imagine what that young boy has had to go through at school.

It seems as if the boy has been unfairly targeted by bullies and had been beaten

a couple of different occasions.

Strangely I hear a knock at my door (surprisingly)

"Hello sir, my name is Shadrach Moore Jr.

are you Detective Sam Hobbes ?"

"Yes"

I reply. "How can I help you ?"

“God told me to come here” he said.

“He told me you could help me”

(Sam narrative)

I was stunned

“How can I be of help to you Shadrach ?”

I asked.

“Dreams… I have dreams and visions that are strong I’m able to remember them for days sometimes months, I believe they come from God he has been giving me dreams for the last 3 months.

“Started with these terrifying horses.”

“Recently I’ve heard voices similar to when God came to Abraham in the Bible.”

“Do you read the Bible Detective ?”

He had a brown backpack that he carried a small laptop in and a few clothes and other things. I guess he uses to do research on.

And a bandage across the right side of his forehead

This kid Shadrach was extremely tough and mature beyond his years. He reminded me of … me.

I thought.

“Shadrach, how old are you ?”

“11, some people think just because I’m a little kid I don’t know anything and discredit everything i have to say, you don’t believe me do you?”

“Yea… well” I say. “I’m sorry Shad please come in and have a seat, are you thirsty ?

”I reply.

Shadrach nodded.

(They both stare at each other)

“So tell me about your most recent dream” I say.

They sit and the Boy began.

"It begins with a huge star coming down out of the sky and it's on fire and it's loud"

"It screams through the sky and hits the earth and causes mass devastation and destruction"

"Fires begin to spread across the world, the death toll is unprecedented, and the water is poisoned."

"Lots of chaos and violence it happens so fast, the masses aren't ready for the impact."

"The staggering thing is everyone sees it .... he begins crying.

"So much ....death."

Shadrach concluded

(Sam dialogue)

"Shad, I saw your story a few weeks ago on the news and you mentioned to the reporter that you knew the boys who were bullying you and that the reason that they picked on you is because you speak to other children about Jesus ? Is that true ?"

"Yes that's true" Shad says. "They were upset at me because.. (slight pause)

I love Jesus and I tell everyone about him."

"I know the boys who harassed me ....they were not good their souls looked shadowy"

he added.

"How do you know ?" I asked

"I can see the inside of the souls of people and sometimes they glow" and he looked at me sincerely "if they are good ..like yours Sam."

I go over and put my hand on his shoulder.

"Hey Shad, it's ok lil bro everything is gonna be alright."

"I'm sorry you have to see those horrific things."

"Im sure there is a reason and with the help of the Lord id like to help you if that's ok with you ?

"He looked up with tears running down his face and a slight smile.

"I'd like that, I don't have any friends, nobody believes me, I feel very alone most days thank you Mr Hobbes."

"You can call me Sam, my hopes are that this is the beginning of a special friendship."

"You're welcome here anytime you want." I say.

(Sam narrates)

Shadrach is a dreamer with powerful dreams from almighty God.

This small unassuming boy had a maturity that was wise beyond his years, and although he didn't have the ability to interpret the meanings of these powerful visions.

he had the wherewithal to seek out help which led him to me.

But He said that God told him to knock on my door ? (Confused)

He can see "Glow" or "Shadow" this was something we could use to our advantage moving forward once we could understand it.

that would help us identify who was friend or foe and I intended on helping him understand this ability more in the days ahead.

Being in the presence of this cool little person was such an honor and I couldn't wait to get him and Dr. Shottah together and see kind of answers we could come up with.

I wonder what Dr. Shottah would think of this special child.

Or what the Old man would say.

I wonder if the forces of evil that we've encountered are aware of this child and how important he is towards stopping them ?

Shad seemed to be relaxed he pulled out a sketch pad and began scribbling on it, he was very detail oriented from what i noticed, drawing and shading as if he didn't have a care in the world.

I didn't want him to pick up on the fact that i was watching him so i kinda acted as if i was concentrating on looking at my phone.

He was enjoying drawing on that paper... it's as if it was some sort of therapy for him, he also began singing very softly and it's in that moment when I realized another talent emerged from this special boy. His voice was very soft but strong at the same time.

so I decided to make a call to Dr. Shottah.

"Hello Dr. I have the Boy Dreamer here and I've had a chance to ask him a few questions about his dreams, he mentioned seeing"

"He mentioned a shooting star

Streaking through the sky leaving a trail of cloud and fire and scorching the earth."

Then suddenly Dr. Shottah. Interrupted me.

"Wormwood." he said very ominously ..He began.

In the Gospel of Luke Chapter twenty-one verse twenty-five, Jesus told us that prior to his return that humanity would see signs in the sun, moon, and stars.

He even went further to say that we would witness great and fearful sights from Heaven.

Sam interrupts respectfully. "Dr. Shottah, what is Wormwood ?"

"Sam this boy dreamer is very important do not let him out of your sight, we will cover that another time."

The image that the boy scribbled sent a chill up my spine.

the Shooting star in Judah's dream had a very ominous feeling the way he looked at me while he was telling me about his dreams absolutely had me convinced it was true.

I thought about my Mom and how she told me that there were chosen people who live among us that have the capability to fight against demonic entities.

As I stood holding the phone listening to Dr. Shottah and watching the Boy scribble the prophetic image he was drawing.

I thought to myself this is the moment she has been preparing me for.

The Old man, Dr. Shottah, the Boy, myself, were what she'd been prophetically calling a "Network"

without her knowing who any of these people were.

Yes, Demons can be killed and Azazel was still out there with others wreaking havoc among humans daily ...monthly... yearly.

Now it was all coming together the right person of the right character with the right knowledge.... all these years she'd been preparing me ...leading me straight into this moment.

I noticed a notification on my phone...

an email from an unknown sender and the title left me wondering what the next step of the journey was heading ... the notification titled was "the Great Gathering."

There is a shortcut that I used to take a few years ago that I always identified with certain memories. It was calm and peaceful and it was rarely used by other drivers... never had any traffic issues or anything like that, one day after I had got done with my workout ..I drove by that little shortcut and noticed that construction workers had begun to deconstruct the structure of the pavement that made it easier to get through to the other end.

It symbolically summed up what my Uncle used to say.

"There are moments that mark your life in two parts, before this and after this."

That path symbolized a lot of things from my past, a lot of memories come to mind when I think about when I use to utilize it.

Now... it's gone like it never happened just like sooo many memories from long ago.

I'll briefly explain this particular moment in my life but it's not an easy one to explain, her name is Ariela Thomas and she was the one that got away.

She was very close to me and we had a very close relationship.

It wasn't perfect of course but it was real.

One thing is certain, that path is gone forever it's almost as if that path never existed.

The past is gone, some paths are closed forever and there is no going back.

www.ingramcontent.com/pod-product-compliance
Lightning Source LLC
LaVergne TN
LVHW052054160826
845678LV00015B/3218

* 9 7 9 8 8 9 5 6 9 6 3 1 6 *